ODYSSEUS AND THE CYCLOPS

A RETELLING BY
Cari Meister

ILLUSTRATED BY
Nadine Takvorian

PICTURE WINDOW BOOKS
a capstone imprint

CAST OF CHARACTERS

ODYSSEUS (OH-DIH-SEE-UHS): Greek king and hero who helped the Greeks win the Trojan War

CYCLOPES (SY-KLOPS): one-eyed giants

POLYPHEMUS (POH-LIH-FEH-MUS): terrible man-eating Cyclops

GREEK SOLDIERS: men who fought under Odysseus in the Trojan War

WORDS TO KNOW

MOUNT OLYMPUS—Greece's highest mountain and the home to the gods of Greek mythology

MYTH—a story told by people in ancient times; myths often tried to explain natural events

TEMPLE—a building used for worship

TROJAN WAR—a mythological 10-year battle between the people of Troy and Greece that began when the Trojan Paris stole the Greek Menelaus' wife, Helen

TROY—a city that some believe existed in what is now western Turkey

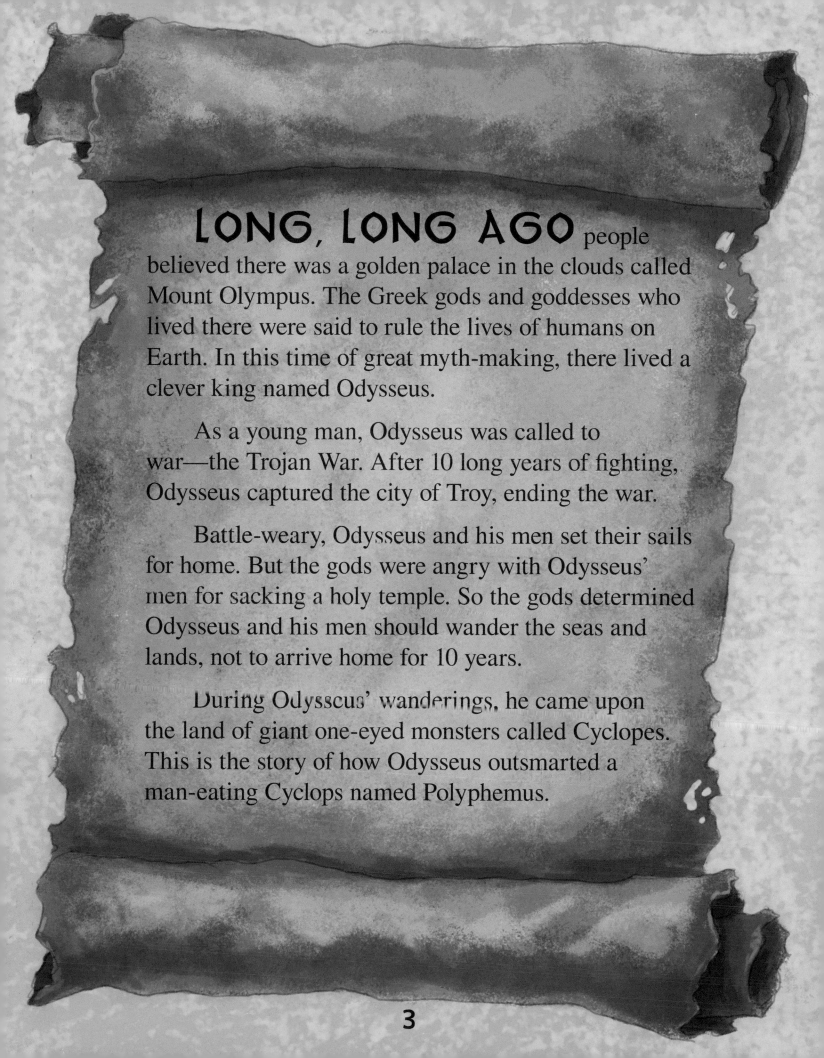

LONG, LONG AGO people
believed there was a golden palace in the clouds called
Mount Olympus. The Greek gods and goddesses who
lived there were said to rule the lives of humans on
Earth. In this time of great myth-making, there lived a
clever king named Odysseus.

As a young man, Odysseus was called to
war—the Trojan War. After 10 long years of fighting,
Odysseus captured the city of Troy, ending the war.

Battle-weary, Odysseus and his men set their sails
for home. But the gods were angry with Odysseus'
men for sacking a holy temple. So the gods determined
Odysseus and his men should wander the seas and
lands, not to arrive home for 10 years.

During Odysseus' wanderings, he came upon
the land of giant one-eyed monsters called Cyclopes.
This is the story of how Odysseus outsmarted a
man-eating Cyclops named Polyphemus.

Odysseus and his ships had been sailing for days without proper food or rest. The men were hungry and tired.

"Perhaps the gods will see fit to send us food and drink for our journey home," said Odysseus.

Shortly thereafter, the ships came upon an island with bleating goats grazing the hills. The men rejoiced as they rowed to shore and readied their bows. Arrow after arrow hit its mark.

Once the Greeks were stuffed full of wild goat, they fell asleep on the island's sandy shore.

The next morning was clear and fair—a perfect day to continue the journey home. The men, happily fed and rested, sang and talked about their wives and children.

But Odysseus was not enjoying the morning with his men. He was curious about what he saw beyond the shore. He saw smoke high up on a craggy mountain. "I wonder who lives there?" he asked.

"I'm not sure," said one of his men. "But it sounds like they keep sheep."

Odysseus strained to hear into the distance. He could hear the faint bleating of sheep and the sound of deep voices.

The soldiers were anxious to continue their journey home. But curiosity held Odysseus like a clenched fist. "I must find out who lives there!" he said.

So Odysseus, along with several of his bravest men, rowed across the bay. Upon reaching the shore, he filled a large goatskin with sweet black wine and said, "A gift for any stranger who shows us kindness!"

The men started the rocky climb up the mountainside. One man who lagged behind said, "I'm not sure about this. Not all strangers are friendly."

After hours of climbing, the Greeks reached a hidden cave. Odysseus pushed through the vines covering the entrance. As the men stepped inside, they gasped. They could hardly believe their eyes!

"Look at the cheese racks!" said one man. "They're overflowing!"

"Every pot is brimming with milk!" said another man.

"This is surely the cave of a very successful shepherd," said Odysseus.

"Let's take as much as we can carry and return to the boat," said a third man.

But Odysseus wouldn't leave. He wanted to meet the shepherd. "We'll stay here until the shepherd returns," he said.

Late that afternoon, the men heard the shepherd whistling. They rushed to the cave's opening to get a better look.

What they saw terrified them more than any battle they had ever fought. Just outside the doorway stood a monstrous one-eyed Cyclops! Even though the giant had not yet reached the cave, the Greeks could smell his stench. Their stomachs heaved. They hid in the shadows in horror.

14

The Cyclops' name was Polyphemus. He was the most vicious of all the Cyclopes on the island. He lumbered in, carrying a large armful of wood for his fire. When he dropped the wood, the cave rumbled. The monster whistled for his sheep and said, "Come in, my fuzzies!"

As the last sheep entered, Polyphemus rolled a boulder over the opening of the cave.

The Greeks were trapped!

"There's no way we can move that boulder," thought Odysseus.

As the men cowered in the corners, Polyphemus went about his work. First he milked the sheep. Then he curdled some of the milk and put it in wicker strainers. He built a roaring fire that lit up the cave. When Polyphemus finally looked up, he saw Odysseus and his men hiding in the shadows.

Polyphemus stood up. "Who are you?" he demanded. The giant stomped his foot. Rocks from the cave's walls cascaded like waves of a waterfall. "Where do you come from?" he asked.

Odysseus stepped forward and answered, "We are Greek soldiers on our way home from a long but successful war. We see you are a great shepherd and would enjoy your hospitality."

The monster laughed. "Hospitality?" he said. "Bah!" He grabbed two men and smashed them on the rocks. Then he opened his huge mouth and ate them. He washed down his meal with milk and fell asleep.

For breakfast, Polyphemus ate two more men. Then he whistled for his sheep. "Come, my fuzzies! Out to pasture," he said.

When all the sheep were out, Polyphemus rolled the boulder over the opening. The men were trapped again.

"It won't be long before we're all eaten," said Odysseus. "We must think of something!"

Odysseus looked around the cave. He saw lambs and sheep pens. He saw cheese on drying racks and milk in clay pots. There was a hill of dung, part of a cart, leather scraps, and shiploads worth of fleece.

Then something caught his eye. At one end of the cave was a long piece of wood. "That's it!" he said. "We'll sharpen that piece of wood and make it red-hot. Then we'll offer the monster wine. After he drinks, he'll sleep. Once he's asleep, we'll attack!"

That afternoon the Cyclops brought in his sheep and closed off the cave. Again he milked the animals, gobbled up two men, and drank his milk.

After Polyphemus was finished, Odysseus filled a large bowl with powerful wine. "Cyclops!" he said. "You've had much man flesh. Try this wine. It's the finest in the world. We hope you'll take pity on us and exchange the wine for our freedom."

The Cyclops grunted, grabbed the bowl, held it up to his big lips, and drank. "Delicious!" he said. "Pour me more!"

Odysseus filled the bowl again. Polyphemus drank. Then he wiped his mouth on a nearby lamb.

"Tell me your name, stranger," Polyphemus said, "and I'll give you a present."

Odysseus was a clever man. He knew it might not be wise to reveal his true name. "My name is Nobody," he said.

"Fill my bowl once more, Nobody," said the Cyclops, "and I will reveal your present."

Again Odysseus filled the giant's bowl with the sweet black wine. The greedy monster drank. Dribbles trickled down the corners of his mouth.

"Hear me, Nobody! This is your present: I'll eat your friends first. Then I'll eat you!" he said as he roared with laughter.

Soon the wine made the giant very sleepy. His eyelid drooped. Then the sound of his body falling to the floor echoed throughout the cave.

When the Greeks were sure he was asleep, they pulled the wooden stake from its hiding place in the dung pile. They brought the sharp, rough tip to the fire and turned it until it was red-hot.

With all their strength, they stabbed the hot stake into the Cyclops' eye. They twisted it around and around.

Polyphemus howled in pain, "My eye! My eye!"

When Polyphemus got to his feet, the men hid. Holding his bloody eye, the wounded Cyclops screamed to his neighbors for help. "Cyclopes! Come help Polyphemus! Nobody has blinded me!"

The other Cyclopes came to the cave's entrance and asked, "What's the matter, Polyphemus?"

"Look what Nobody did to me!" Polyphemus yelled. "Nobody blinded me!"

"Well," said the other Cyclopes, "if nobody hurt you, your misfortune must have been brought on by the gods. We cannot help you." And they left.

Polyphemus' entire face turned purple. He gnashed his teeth and stomped his feet, triggering a small earthquake inside the cave.

The next morning Polyphemus pushed away the boulder from the cave's opening. He sat down and held up his bloodstained hands. "This is the only way out!" he boomed. "There's no escaping. I'll crush you when you try to leave."

As the sheep left, Polyphemus felt the top of each one. The men couldn't ride the sheep out of the cave.

That afternoon, as the giant waited by the door, Odysseus schemed. The leather scraps he had seen in the cave gave him an idea.

The next morning Polyphemus rolled back the large boulder to let out his sheep. Once again, he patted them down, one by one.

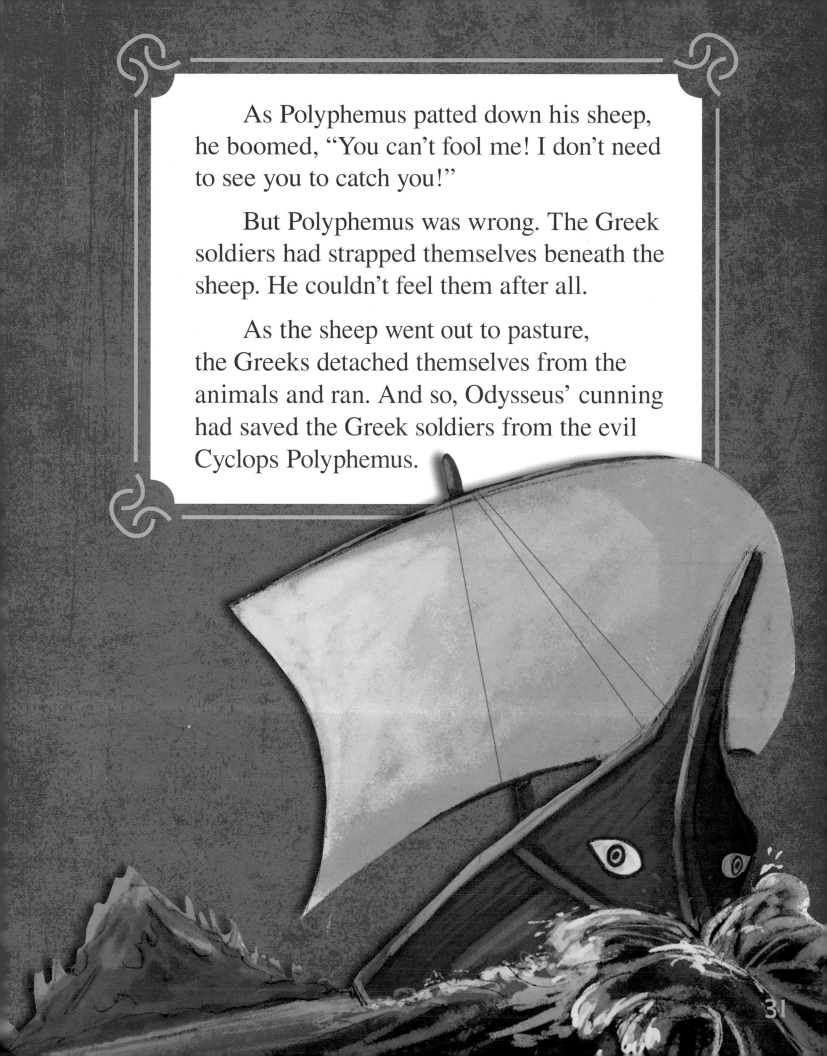

As Polyphemus patted down his sheep, he boomed, "You can't fool me! I don't need to see you to catch you!"

But Polyphemus was wrong. The Greek soldiers had strapped themselves beneath the sheep. He couldn't feel them after all.

As the sheep went out to pasture, the Greeks detached themselves from the animals and ran. And so, Odysseus' cunning had saved the Greek soldiers from the evil Cyclops Polyphemus.

READ MORE

Cooper, Gilly Cameron. *Odysseus and the Cyclops*. Graphic Greek Myths and Legends. Milwaukee, Wis.: World Almanac Library, 2007.

Curlee, Lynn. *Mythological Creatures: A Classical Bestiary: Tales of Strange Beings, Fabulous Creatures, Fearsome Beasts, & Hideous Monsters from Greek Mythology*. New York: Atheneum Books for Young Readers, 2008.

Tracy, Kathleen. *Odysseus*. Hockessin, Del.: Mitchell Lane Publishers, 2009.

INTERNET SITES

FactHound offers a safe, fun way to find Internet sites related to this book. All of the sites on FactHound have been researched by our staff.

Here's all you do:

Visit *www.facthound.com*

Type in this code: 9781404866669

Super-cool stuff! Check out projects, games and lots more at
www.capstonekids.com

LOOK FOR ALL THE BOOKS IN THE GREEK MYTHS SERIES:

THE BATTLE OF THE OLYMPIANS AND THE TITANS

JASON AND THE ARGONAUTS

MEDUSA'S STONY STARE

ODYSSEUS AND THE CYCLOPS

PANDORA'S VASE

THE WOODEN HORSE OF TROY

Thanks to our adviser for his expertise and advice:
Terry Flaherty, PhD
Professor of English
Minnesota State University, Mankato

Editor: Shelly Lyons
Designer: Alison Thiele
Art Director: Nathan Gassman
Production Specialist: Sarah Bennett
The illustrations in this book were created with pencil.

Picture Window Books
1710 Roe Crest Drive
North Mankato, MN 56003
877-845-8392
www.capstonepub.com

 All books published by Picture Window Books are manufactured with paper containing at least 10 percent post-consumer waste.

Library of Congress Cataloging-in-Publication Data
Meister, Cari.
  Odysseus and the cyclops : a retelling / by Cari Meister ; illustrated by Nadine Takvorian.
    p. cm. — (Greek myths)
  Includes index.
  ISBN 978-1-4048-6666-9 (library binding)
  1. Odysseus (Greek mythology)—Juvenile literature.
  2. Mythology, Greek—Juvenile literature. I. Takvorian, Nadine. II. Title.
  BL820.O3.M45 2011
  398.20938'02—dc22
                                    2011006989

Printed in the United States of America in North Mankato, Minnesota.   102014   008497R